Vicki L. Wille

Think Act Prosper

&

Success Will Find You

How to Become a Lifelong Investor

Also by the Author

Randee Leads a Charmed Life: Traditions Taught by a Father
by Vicki Silberberger

Four Secrets to Successful Investing:
A Primer that Will Make Anyone a Smarter Investor
by Vicki L. Wille

ISBN 9781500298326

Printed in the United States of America

Dedicated

to all of you who are willing to

change your thinking and manifest personal prosperity.

Contents

Foreword

Introduction

part one | Think: To believe something is
true.

part two | Act: To bring about a change.

part three | Prosper: To put into effect your
decision to change.

part four | More Tools for Implementing
What You're Learning

part five | Money and Wealth

Biography

Acknowledgements

Foreword

In the spring of 2013, I was introduced to Professor Thomas L. Jackson, a 40-year tenured professor of business at the College of Southern Nevada. During the course of our first meeting, he asked if I would be willing to speak to students in one of his classes.

Although I had not spoken to a group in years, I was honored by his request. When I asked if he had a specific topic in mind, he explained that he had been inviting various speakers to share their top three rules for success. I accepted his gracious invitation without hesitation.

I spent hours preparing materials for the students. This consisted of *my three rules*, the details for each supported by famous quotes and references. I wanted to keep it academic, yet relevant to the outside world.

Professor Jackson eased my way by explaining to his students the etiquette of attending such lectures, especially the appropriateness of sending emailed thank you notes to speakers who have taken time to prepare and share their knowledge with the class. I was stunned to find at least half of these students had sent me emails describing the impact *My Three Rules for Success* presentation made on them.

Within days of my lecture, Professor Jackson called to ask if I had time to speak to his remaining five classes. In a bit of a daze, I agreed. But it didn't end there. During the next six months, the professor requested I speak to 12 more classes, which meant I eventually spoke to over 585 people. I continued to be amazed by the volume of emailed feedback.

I read every one of the students' emails and I noticed a recurring theme: They all told me I had touched them in one way or another. These students were hungry for more information than I would be able to provide during a regular speaking presentation. Perhaps a book was in order, one that could educate them about the power of thought and their ability to create ideas, coupled with the responsibility to implement and share these ideas. I believe this is how certain things in the material world come into existence.

I thank Professor Jackson for requesting I present *My Three Rules for Success* to his classes, and hope that my experiences, knowledge, and wisdom will aid others in recognizing and implementing their desires for prosperity in their own lives.

Vicki L. Wille
Las Vegas, Nevada
June 21, 2014

INTRODUCTION

Success is such a simple, yet impactful word. The notion of success certainly varies from person to person. Yes, each and every one of us has a very different definition of what it means to be successful. So you will need to ask yourself a couple of questions before we start:

- Do you give yourself credit for the success-ful actions you have already completed?

- Or are you measuring your value in such a way that you have convinced yourself you are not worthy of success?

Before I begin sharing the message from which I believe my prosperity is built, please allow me to share a little bit about my journey, how my personal successes began, and where they have led me. In this way I can tell you how I know I will continue to have even more wonderful life experiences and continue to prosper.

I developed and defended a flawed belief system in my earlier years that kept confirming "I am never going to amount to much of anything." I came from an upper-middle class family, but I was not formally educated. I did not think I was either pretty or intelligent, and I was sickly for most of my childhood. In other words, I already believed I had nothing to offer anyone. A man I dated in my early 20s drove that point home by telling me I needed to "find some kind of job" which would support me because I would "never amount to anything." The seeds I had already planted were now germinating because of this man and other people like him.

Into adulthood, I continued to struggle with my health and lack of self-esteem. I eventually met a man I thought accepted me and saw me as an attractive and smart woman. After a short courtship, we married and moved across the country to Seattle. I really thought life was going to be different. I was not yet cognizant of the fact that no matter where I moved, all my old thoughts, doubts, and inhabitations would come with me. These things resided in my head; so no matter where I went, there I was.

I soon became pregnant, but miscarried. My husband offered me no comfort through this experience and I should have realized then he was showing me exactly who he was.

As these things sometimes happen, in no time at all I found I was pregnant again. Like so many young women of my generation, I had no idea who I was, let alone what I wanted out of life. I was just floating along in space and time, pretending all was okay. I had no idea what challenges could be lying along my path in life. Why should I? I was not thinking. I was just dealing with life as I stumbled along.

Staying true to the soap opera I had been writing for my young self, a few months later I discovered my husband was being unfaithful. I felt betrayed and trapped. My pregnancy was difficult and I was having other health issues. My stubborn pride insisted I make my own decisions. Embarrassment over my perceived failures caused me to project my parents' disappointment in me, which in turn prevented me from talking with them. I once again proved to myself that I had nothing to offer anyone.

Maybe it was Divine Intervention when Howard, the manager and owner of our apartment complex, came over that day to check on something in our apartment. Howard sensed I was unhappy and, in his fatherly way, suggested we go to his apartment to talk.

Howard knew how to ask questions without being intrusive. He encouraged me to share and, after listening to my story, he provided some much needed insight. He pointed out that God was already working miracles in my life. The first one was the fact that I was pregnant, and what a privilege and honor that should be for any woman! Then he reminded me that my husband had just been chosen by his company to relocate to Chicago, all expenses paid. He pointed out the added bonus: this would place me within a few hours of my parents and a sister.

"You see," said Howard, "God provides ways to make life easy. It is our own lack of belief which brings about all the pain and struggle." He hugged me and reminded me that I was stronger than I knew.

His amazing support, wisdom, and kindness inspired me to build up my strength and begin to focus on the end result. I could do this. I really could do this.

I kept reminding myself that by the end of the month I would be within a short distance of my family.

As soon as we arrived in Chicago I contacted my parents and arranged to visit for the Christmas holidays. I went on ahead, alone. After a few days of being with my parents, I explained how unhappy I was, how my husband had cheated on me, and confessed my desire to stay with them and not return to Chicago.

My father suggested we refrain from making any final decisions until my husband joined us for Christmas. I did not understand this. I was his daughter, his loyalties should lie with me, and yet he wanted to hear what *my husband* had to say? Why? I would not fully understand the *why* for some time, but I came to understand more as the knowledge of my own character grew.

When my husband arrived, he had the audacity to bring the woman he had been sleeping with! She had followed us to Chicago! He reasoned, "I thought it would be okay for me to ask her to come, since she had nowhere else to go."

My father's reaction was swift and final. He told my husband and the woman to leave at once. He informed him that immediately after Christmas they would be helping me move out of the apartment and I would come to stay with them. Now I realized my father's personal need to see what kind of man my husband really was. And once he saw, he had no doubts about what needed to be done.

Due to my pregnancy, I was unable to get a job to cover my expenses. My mother offered to pay me to do the housework and grocery shopping. Using my hands always made me feel valuable, so this option felt right. I even offered to cook all the meals. Besides, it wasn't like I had a big social life or anything else to do. Except maybe I was starting to learn how to think differently about myself.

These small actions had a profound effect on me. In time I would recognize the work I did at my parents' home was aiding in the building of my self-esteem. I was learning how to deal with responsibility, structure, organization, and—most importantly of all—showing respect and gratitude to my parents.

I kept the momentum building through the birth of my daughter. Soon after, I found a job which provided the means to move into a duplex a few blocks from my parents' house. My mother told me about a nice lady who cared for small children. After meeting with her, I felt assured my little Monica would thrive in that loving environment.

I settled into my new life and even began to feel I had the freedom to think about building new friendships. I dated once in a while, just to have a social life of some kind, but I was soured on the idea of marrying again.

My mother had other ideas. She wanted me to be married. At that time she was selling real estate, to pilots in particular, and she was determined to find me a husband. She wasn't successful at this; however, a friend of mine was. She introduced me to a young, educated, and successful fighter pilot named Frank. To my mother's contentment, it was not long before we were engaged.

It was not a love match. But he seemed to care about my daughter and that carried a lot of weight with me. I did not trust my own instincts after my first marriage attempt. Frank seemed to meet most of the criteria I thought were important at the time. I did like his brains and his family was stable. I think he thought he was marrying into money; he had no idea my parents had saved for 20 years so they could build their dream house. Truth was, I had come from regular folks, just as he had.

One month prior to the wedding, I told Frank I thought maybe we should wait a while. It felt like we were moving too fast. Frank told me I was just nervous and all would be fine. True to my nature, I listened to my man and discounted my own feelings. After all, he was a college graduate and fighter pilot, and I was … well, not much of anything. Despite the changes I had begun to make, I was still just going with the flow, following the crowd. I did not realize I was not *thinking* about my dreams and desires, what I wanted in life. I was existing and little else.

Frank adopted Monica shortly after we married. Over the next few years, I gave birth to two sons, Brandt and Byron. Unfortunately, it took me a while to realize that Frank only had two great aspirations: being a fighter pilot and drinking with the guys.

About five years into the marriage, I admitted to myself that I was not happy. With three children and no formal education beyond high school, I felt alone and trapped. My oldest son had many health issues (asthma on top of bone and kidney disorders). How could I provide special care for him if I had to work? In my heart of hearts, I knew my primary responsibility was to my children. Realizing I was unhappy was the easy part; what was hard was discovering what could make me happy. Casting about for solutions, I started reading autobiographies of successful people and studied various how-to books. Many of the latter were on handicrafts, like how to upholster furniture. In addition to reading, I joined bridge clubs just to get out and meet people.

It had not occurred to me that, by these simple actions, I was beginning to live life instead of just existing. I was actually developing talents. I was creating useful pictures in my head of success by completing projects, learning to build relationships, picking up knowledge from others, and, yes, even building my math and communication skills through playing bridge. I was becoming a *real* person.

A hard fact of military life meant moving every three to five years. Time eventually came for Frank to receive another new assignment. One evening he came home elated, announcing he had been selected to fly the new F-16 aircraft. There were only a handful of pilots who had been given this honor, and I shared his pride and excitement. Despite the hubbub, I had the presence of mind to ask when and where we would be moving. Taking part in the plans gave me a sense of value and focus.

We were initially moved to Hill Air Force Base in Utah. However, when they discovered there had been an over-assignment at that base, Frank was one of three pilots reassigned to Las Vegas. After only six months in Utah, we were off again to a new city.

The children and I went ahead to Las Vegas to establish the home and arrange their schooling. I'll never forget coming over the hill and seeing Las Vegas for the first time. Mixed in with the anticipation was an abiding calmness. It was as though I was finally home … and safe.

The kids and I settled into the house, schools, and a routine. Frank arrived a few days before Christmas and the family was back together again. A more accurate description would be that the players were back together. Lying dormant, just beneath the surface, was a widening divide between Frank and the family.

Within a year it became obvious that our finances were doing poorly. Frank was charging a lot at the Officers' Club, which forced me to charge on the credit card for basic family needs. He didn't wake up to the fact that we needed more money until he tried to use the card to buy a pair of cowboy boots and it was declined. Yet he accepted no responsibility for our situation.

I told Frank that I was willing to get a job. It would be the next day before he addressed my offer and replied, "I give you permission." Those words stuck in my head and still remain with me. *Who was he to give me permission?* It was clear to me that I not only *needed* to work, but that I *wanted* to work. It wasn't just to provide better care for my children. There was something else coming to the surface in my life.

Indeed, God works in such fascinating ways.

One Friday I went along with Frank to visit the Officers' Club. That's when I met Barbara. She fascinated me. She had studied law, but did not enjoy the practice, so became a stockbroker at Paine Weber. Our conversation left me thinking about what type of job I wanted. I realized I wasn't interested in a *job*, I wanted a *position* that could lead me into a *career* ... something that would become a part of me and I could use wherever we lived.

The following Monday I called Barbara and told her about my recently defined needs to work. I wanted her opinion regarding paralegal school. She shared her thoughts and I thanked her.

Before long I received a call from Chic, the assistant to the branch manager at Paine Weber where Barbara worked. She said that Barbara had referred me and she wanted to know if I would accept a receptionist position. I hadn't worked in ten years and my résumé had little to recommend me—lacking a degree or any training—so I jumped at the offer. I did not care about the rate of pay; I just wanted to work in an environment where I could grow.

Then I realized I didn't have an appropriate work wardrobe. I called my parents, told them the situation, and requested a loan to buy a few outfits. They sent me the money with a simple promissory note. My parents understood the value of teaching lessons of responsibility, even to their adult daughter.

Monday arrived and I was so nervous. My first day must have gone well, because on Tuesday I was taken to lunch by Chic and she told me they would like to offer me a sales assistant position working with the top three brokers, as well as an increase in pay.

I could hardly believe my good fortune. This rapid series of opportunities was expanding my definction of belief in my self. I began to understand and accept that I am smart, have the ability to learn, am open, and willing to take risks.

James, a Harvard graduate and one of the three brokers I worked for, called me into his office to dictate a letter. Out of necessity, I had developed my own little version of shorthand, and it served me well enough. However, on this occasion he repeatedly used 13-letter words that I had to keep asking him to spell out. I went to my desk and typed up the draft. After looking up definitions of the words, I substituted familiar words or phrases and submitted the typed draft to him. He was furious and instructed me to retype it exactly as he dictated.

I took him his version and, as he signed it, I said, "You will lose clients because you are intimidating them." He didn't respond. Within the month, three clients left. And he was furious yet again.

I got up the nerve to explain the dynamics to him: His clients are his clients because they understand their businesses and they know how to make money doing what they do. But investing is unfamiliar and confusing to them. His habit of using words they could not understand only made matters worse. It scared them. He asked me to explain why I thought I understood his clients better than he. I simply replied, "I know because I am the one who *talks with them*."

As my sense of self-worth at work grew, I began to recognize the signs of how Frank treated me at home. He seemed to think he was better than me. Our disagreements were occurring more and more frequently. He was staying at the Officers' Club more often. I was becoming aware that he was not even trying to act as if he wanted to be involved with our children.

Acting. That thought stuck with me. It was as though we were actors in a play. The children and I were playing our parts to satisfy Frank's need to show the world the valiant test pilot had an all-American family. Behind the scenes, I was becoming more and more confident in my ability to raise the children on my own. I began recalling incidents of people I knew staying in bad situations. As I compared them to my own life, I saw no value in this. It was unfair to all parties involved.

Once again, God came to my rescue. Frank was given short orders for a one-year assignment in Montgomery, Alabama, to attend the Air Command and Staff Program. This was another great honor for him. However, I didn't think the family should go. I explained that it was unfair to uproot the children for only one year. He should go alone, and we would remain in Las Vegas. Within eight weeks he was off to Montgomery.

By the end of the first month of his leaving, laughter was reverberating off the walls of the house. The atmosphere was relaxed and fun. So, this is how it could be! I knew the time had come to begin planning for a divorce. Time came for Frank's return and I decided to send the children to their grandparents' home. I expected the divorce would be an ugly process and they did not need to witness their parents going through it.

Frank arrived home and came up to kiss me … and he knew. We talked for hours. He cried and promised he would be different. He called and asked a friend to come and speak with me. When the friend arrived, I explained what I had tried to tell Frank, "We are on different tracks and staying together would only destroy us and our children." Frank did not expect his friend to understand and agree with my argument. He told Frank it was indeed time to divorce.

Allowing a few days for Frank to get used to the idea, he finally admitted it would be the best for all involved. Before the children returned home, we settled him into an apartment and I filed for divorce. Within a month of our first talk on the subject, the divorce was finalized. Speedy divorces: one of the perks of living in Nevada that hadn't previously occurred to me.

The children came home and adjusted well. I was a little surprised at how quickly Frank took to being single. Inside another month, he was in a new relationship and remarried soon after.

As for me, I focused on taking the required exams to become a stockbroker. I was very excited upon learning I had passed and assumed they would waste no time in moving me from sales assistant to a broker's position. That didn't happen. I couldn't see it at the time, but after a few years I realized my lack of promotion had actually been a blessing.

One of the brokers I worked for agreed to assist me in applying at other firms. He recognized my talents and thought I should be using them as a broker. With his assistance, I interviewed at three firms and was hired by the firm where I most wanted to work. It is true that allowing others to see your talents and asking them for their guidance is one of the most valuable tools anyone can have.

Eight years into my career as a broker, an opportunity at a new type of license came about. This allowed the licensee to not only manage the client's money, but also maintain discretion over which investments would be best suited to the investment counselor's style. It is called a Series 65. I attended the first class that was offered and passed the exam. This new tool in my bag of miracles would ultimately separate me from the other brokers. True, it placed more responsibility and accountability on me, but I welcomed this.

As I was growing in knowledge of my talents, interests, and abilities, I became aware of and reflected upon the energies we carry with us—that these energies attract the same kinds of energy. If I was doubting and unsure, I would attract doubtful and unsure people towards me. If I believed in illness, I would become ill. As I thought things through along these lines, my beliefs in the power of God and the energies of life expanded as well. For instance, when I opened up to new information regarding spiritual concepts of energy, I was exposed to *Feng Shui*, the ancient Chinese system considered to govern spatial arrangement and orientation as relating to the flow of natural energy.

The more I read about *Feng Shui*, I felt compelled to search for a practitioner. I asked around, to people I thought might know such things, and was referred to Linda. She came to my office, drew out the space, and told me what I needed to rearrange and explained the reasoning behind it.

I implemented the changes and was stunned by the quick changes in my energy. Within a month my production began to increase and continued to rise exponentially. I moved my assistant's desk from its original position and his health issues rapidly improved. He was so surprised when he realized he was no longer feeling ill all the time, he invited Linda's *Feng Shui* into his apartment.

I was happy in my personal and family life and everything was working well. So when life again threw me a curveball—as life seems to insist upon doing—I hoped I was ready. And this one seemed daunting. The firm was now telling me I had to alter my investment style. However, their new demands would have created horrible tax consequences for my clients. So I consulted with an attorney and he recommend I open up my own company and take my clients with me.

I was not mentally prepared for such a move. Consistent with the many other incidents that had led up to this moment, I felt God intervening once again. It became abundantly clear: If I wanted to keep my practice, I would have no choice but to follow the attorney's advice. Over the next few weeks I spent hours preparing the best I could. I called my CPA and requested her to fill out the SEC and IRS requirements while I prepared to open up my firm and move my clients. With the help of four assistants, long hours, and arduous work, my new company, Randolph & Associates, was up and running.

After spending more than a quarter century managing money for clients, I still look forward to meeting new people, discovering new investment opportunities, and building long-term relationships. Randolph continues to grow thanks to my desire to help others become prosperous.

······

Through the years I have allowed more of my talents to be developed. I created a card game called *It's SoLow*; authored *Randee Leads a Charmed Life* and *The Four Secrets to Successful Investing*; became active in public speaking; and recently launched *SuccessEnomics.com – The Art of Creating Wealth*.

I share the points and evolution of my journey with you to demonstrate my realization that there are no straight shots to success. The parts of the foundation of success are created through *thought* mixed with *action* and *implementation*.

THINK: To believe something is true.

Our minds are perhaps the most valuable asset we possess as humans. More than the organ known as the brain, it is through our minds that we develop the skill to think critically; communicate clearly; and learn to analyze and process the information we receive.

Throughout history, there have been those who have understood the power of the mind and have been able to mold the thinking of others. Great religious leaders, kings, and statesmen understood and practiced this. They knew then as we know now: People act as they think, and will also react to the thoughts of others—especially when those thoughts are stronger and more convincing than their own.

I invite you to consider the concept that, beyond basic survival instincts, all your needs and desires are first created in your mind. From there, everything is governed by your mind's thoughts. If allowed and nourished, they seem to *take on an unstoppable life of their own*. Based on your own thinking, you create—or have created—everything that comes or does not come to you.

You can create such a strong mental atmosphere of success that its power of attraction will be irresistible. You can send your thoughts around the world and have them bring back to you whatever you desire. You can fill your place of business with so much power of success that it will draw even more business from near and far.

The first step is to empty your mind of all unbelief. To be clear, please know that I am writing with the hope of teaching those who have the capacity to *believe*. For those who believe, it will manifest in their lives.

It is important to understand that without clear thinking on the part of the thinker, no real creative work can be done. Like attracts like. As water seeks its own level, so do our minds and thoughts bring us only those things we inherently believe. We are always a reflection of our thoughts. Even though they may be bringing us undesired events, those events are the direct representation of our thoughts.

In order to get ahead, develop self-esteem, and create a life full of success, it is up to *you* and *only you* to take control of your mind and allow only beneficial thoughts. This does not mean to isolate or deny participation in life; it only means that *you should not internalize* words, pictures, and sounds that offer no substantial value or benefit.

Remember, the answer lies within each of you if you will only take the time to be quiet and listen to the Power that created all.

One of the challenges we all must face some time or another is how we handle failure. After a few failed attempts do you find yourself believing you are unworthy and your failures only prove this? Or have you recognized that you needed to alter your course by a tiny amount to get back on track?

Over the years I have observed people who have become closed-minded; they push people away due to their own poor attitudes while truly believing that they are the healthy ones. Our minds are our engines and they drive our journeys towards success; it is our souls that keep our passions alive. Be careful not to allow your mind to steer too far to one extreme or the other—because happiness surely lies somewhere in the middle.

Every time you think, you are setting in motion a power that creates. The results it will bring will be based on specific thoughts you add to it. During the thinking process, when you create an idea, the mind creates it for you and places it on your path of life. Make your thoughts become your greatest friends. Your thoughts are always with you 24/7. Your thoughts never desert you. Do not allow your mind to wander to places of doubt, fear, or wondering about the *what ifs* of life. Train your thoughts, because your thoughts will give you back exactly what you truly believe.

The Power of Words

The words you speak are a representation of your mind's thoughts. So many have heard about the *power of words*, but few take the time to truly comprehend what this means and how it comes about.

It begins by thinking the words, coming to believe them, and then those words ultimately will attract to you whatever you believe.

Consider this: If you believe you are stupid, incapable, unworthy, or useless, then you will attract people who treat you as though you actually are those things. However, if you believe you are a brilliant, capable, worthy individual, and offer the world great value and purpose, you will be seen as that person.

Getting there. The following points are offered as a method to begin teaching yourself to think constructively:

- Allow the words you think to be a true reflection of your spirit, for as these become spoken words they will continue to nourish your beliefs.

- Allow no space in your mind for doubt and negativity.

- Thoughts must never be taken for granted or ignored, for they are creating your life as you live it. Keep in mind: *Nothing* can happen to us that is not first an accepted belief of our own consciousness. We may not always be aware of what is going on within, but with practice and new habits we are able to control our thoughts, more and more, until we are automatically able to think about what we want, regardless of the perceived reality of any situation.

- Give conviction and strength to your words. When you are strong in your conviction, your words will be an outward expression of your thoughts and spirit.

It is important to constantly be cognizant of the thoughts that run through your head, the words you speak, and the words and actions of those with whom you associate. When you begin your new path towards creating success, you will notice that many of your old associations will need to be left behind. Accepting that you attract your thoughts, you will begin to change your belief from one of lacking towards one of prosperity and your old habits and associations will need to be altered accordingly.

When you continually work at altering and developing your beliefs and thoughts, you will notice real changes in your life. Just like a sports player, entertainer, or any successful person will tell you: Daily focus on your talents, dreams, and desires is a requirement. The key to all success is staying aware of your own thoughts and confirming what you know to be true inside yourself.

Early on in my journey to discovering the power which I had within me, I wrote down all I wanted to receive. I designed the basic house I wanted, pictured the car I wanted, and so on. I put down dates which I thought were reasonable to obtain these goals. Since my savings were next to nothing, I decided on five years for the car and 20 years for the house.

Well, time passed and I saw some of my smaller requests quickly come to fruition: a nice sofa, a functioning TV, a new pair of work heels. When I would get these items, I realized what I thought about was what was being attracted to me. So I continued to read and exercise my thinking and my beliefs.

In less than half the time I had originally estimated, my house came to me. One day, my manager mentioned in passing that he and his family had just purchased three houses in Rancho Circle. I thought nothing more of it as I was focused on other needs with him at that moment. Then, a few days later, I was driving to work and I heard a voice which said *very clearly*, "Move into the center of the city or commit suicide." I remember thinking, "You don't give me much choice."

When I arrived at work I went to the manager and asked if he still had the three houses and if any were in my price range. He said they were and by 10:00 that very morning I was out looking at them. There it was! The house I had drawn out 15 years before. It had come to me five years earlier than I planned. I got a loan and purchased it. It needed some work, to be sure, but over the next two years I made the improvements that brought it up to my idea of a dream home.

As a further example, my original list had a *Mercedes* for my dream car, but that was because a Mercedes was the only luxury car I knew about at the time. When the time came to purchase my luxury car, I had kept an open mind and discovered that a Lexus was really my car of choice.

To this day, I ask for what I want ... but I am careful how I go about it. Not concerned with the mere material things in life as proof of my success, I am more interested in sharing my knowledge through various avenues which allow me to help those who assist me as well as those who receive my information.

We all need to have a *backbone* instead of a *wishbone*. When you pay attention to the *knowing* you have inside, you allow for the time and opportunities necessary to bring your internal capabilities to life. Your spirit houses the *knowing*—when it is not allowed expression, you can be sure it will remind you by keeping you off balance.

Visualize. As you practice visualization, it's best to begin by defining the end results of your vision. See yourself at the end of your life looking back and recognizing all the things you have accomplished during your life. See the family you created, houses you lived in, cars you drove, investments you made, businesses you built, and more. Be proud and congratulate yourself for persevering through all the obstacles that were thrown in your way. Remind yourself that it was through the power of your thoughts you were able to accomplish all your dreams and desires.

When you give your thoughts direction, your thoughts create a kind of roadmap to follow. You are already going *somewhere* and becoming *something*; so why not take the time now to get to know yourself and choose what *YOU* really want out of life. For example, what if you live in Los Angeles and want to go to New York City? If you give no thought to planning a route, you could end up zigzagging across the country and may never get there. However, if you take the time to think about which route is best suited for your needs, you will discover you not only accomplish your goal, but also enjoy the journey.

The challenge most people face is stating that they *wish* to live a life full of their desires; however, they take little or no time to investigate, research, and learn how to create the life they claim to want. Those who do develop a plan often discover that hard work, dedication, and persistence are not just suggestions, they are essential requirements. Many then decide the effort of the journey is just too much.

Choosing

Your thoughts must be based on the belief that each individual has the *power of choice*. Once you choose—if you are willing to do the work and persevere through all of the challenges—the mind will begin to create and keep the fire of your spirit alive. It may not manifest in the timeframe you wish, or in the way you plan; but if you pray on it, see it, take focused action, and implement the plan, you will receive what you desire. In other words, you will prosper.

You need to know exactly what it is that you are wishing for and make the perfect mental picture of it. You must absolutely believe that you already have it and never do or say anything that is contrary or denies it. Tell no one about your true desires. Have you ever noticed how sometimes you have a thought that really moves you, but when you try to tell someone, it loses all its specialness? I'm reminded of Bette Midler's saying, "The worst part of *success* is to try finding someone who is happy for you."

Life is to be lived and your bounty should be shared. When you share and give your time and talents for the benefit of others, you will discover that your life begins to move in positive directions. It is through this process that people begin to discover their capabilities.

There is a saying, "Walk the walk, don't just talk the talk." Think about this a moment. How many times have you met someone who really inspires you, and then you eventually discover he or she was all talk and no action? When you begin to build new relationships, notice if they are willing to share their talents and the abilities they claim to have, or if they only *give* when they expect to *receive* something in return, either an action (like a favor or some kind of work) or money. Once you begin to work or socialize with them, you will uncover a lot about who they are. You might discover that their words match their actions, that their moral character is one you may honor and trust—or perhaps not.

People are the foundation of life, so it follows that the material progress we all enjoy was created through the imaginations or thought processes of others. When we learn about others, we learn about ourselves. Teach yourself by discovering worlds of which you have been unaware. Perhaps you could begin by noticing others who are of a totally different economic status. When you question, investigate, and research what their worlds are all about and understand what drives them, during the process you may uncover more talents within yourself. You need to stop observing and begin to participate in all aspects of life.

I am a business thinker. Business has always been my driving force. But that's not all there is in my life. Allow me to explain:

There's another side of me that enjoys creating crafty and imaginative things for my family's pleasure. I have as much fun doing them as reaping the end results. When my children were young, I sewed stuffed animals and made their rooms look like a circus by using window dressings, bedspreads, and even paintings on the walls. My daughter's bedroom was pink and frilly with a handmade quilt I made from pink fabric she liked.

Even as I began to write this, I had been spending time making Christmas stockings for my daughter and grandson to have at their home for the holidays. I have made my own patterns for items they enjoy, like a guitar and microphone for my daughter and *Thomas the Train* for my grandson. I added hand-sewn sequins, beads, and bells to bring their stockings to life. I learned these things from watching my mother when I was a child. None of this is hard; it only takes a desire to make and take the time. There's no reason to feel defeated before you begin, convinced that only especially talented people are capable of doing these things. *Each of us* has the ability to find the solutions to accomplish anything we can think we would enjoy and thereby change our lives by following through.

All three of my children live in the artistic world. My daughter, Monica, has cooked under famous chefs, attended the Fashion Institute of Technology in New York City, and works to learn natural remedy cures. These are three very different disciplines for which she has passions to learn. Each of these opportunities gave her tools to discover her true talents and interests, and she found a way to combine them. These days she teaches others how to heal their bodies with foods and color therapy, all while finishing up her degree. She's also working on a theatrical performance piece that aids others in unleashing their own unique, creative abilities.

My second child, Brandt, chose to work in the entertainment industry. He directs, edits, and produces commercials, music videos, and movies. He has even acted in several movies. He has more interest in business than his brother and sister, but his main desires and dreams are in the arts.

Bryon, my youngest, is a scientific thinker. He has grown hundreds of cactus plants, many of which were started from seeds. His focus is on having his own nursery. He has written books on the different species and plans to travel the world to learn more about their native environments and values. His hobby is painting —and he has created many pieces, which he sells whenever he chooses.

Now, getting back to my point of sharing all this with you, it was not until 2004 that I began to integrate my creative side with my business life. I surprised myself when, by opening up to my creativity, I learned more about what my children were thinking and working on. The result has further expanded my own thinking and contributed to a feeling of a truly balanced life. I relax more, for one thing. And a bonus is that as I have become more curious and developed a respect for those who are different from me—even though different on the surface, I seldom have to dig very far to discover we hold similar character strengths and moral codes.

This awareness allows me to view life through a special lens, as I have learned that each of us is entitled to express our thoughts with a unique style. I discovered I needed to accept, respect, and honor the choices and talents of others; just as I have learned the importance and value of honoring and respecting my own unique contributions.

Attitude

Expressed in many different ways, attitude is most commonly found through speaking, especially through the inflections and choice of words. Outward appearances and the nonverbal communications we display—like the way we carry ourselves, sit, or stand—are also expressions of our attitude. Our appearance is a reflection of our inner thoughts and beliefs.

To those who make it their business to read others (and to professional gamblers here in Las Vegas, believe me, it *is* a business)—to understand how people act and react—this is often called a "tell." The tell is what we need to recognize in ourselves, especially when observing others.

Do you know your tell? Are you confident in your convictions, morals, and beliefs? When you walk in a room are you comfortable, relaxed, and smiling, hoping to meet new people? Or do you walk in and immediately look for someone you know so you can sit with him or her and just get the event over with?

Remember, your thoughts are projected from your body as well as your words. You need to develop and possess the knowledge that, at this very moment, you are the best version of all that you can be. This is nothing new. Aristotle was aware of it when he pointed out to his pupils, "How we long to become that which we already are." Each step you take out of your comfort zone towards your dreams will aid you in the knowledge that you already possess within you all the desired qualities and talents, and you are projecting them on the outside as well.

Exercises. Once you understand that your *mind* is your *power*, you will become secure in the knowledge that you need only feed it healthy, positive thoughts—while you continue to block negative thoughts—in order to become the person you desire to be. An exercise I did in my late thirties helped me find and open a vast amount of "space" in my head. I took the story of my life as I saw it, up to that point—all the old, negative thoughts along with all the fun, loving, caring, supportive thoughts—and mentally threw them all to the ground. They looked like pieces of a jigsaw puzzle. Then I watched myself as I bent over and picked up only the pieces of my life's puzzle that I wanted to keep. The fun, loving, caring, exciting, positive events were placed back in my mind. This gave me a new foundation or framework from which to start the rest of my life.

You see, I recognized that while I am not perfect, I am a human being in the process of living a life. I thought about all of the people from my past (parents, siblings, friends, teachers, ministers, co-workers, and everyone who touched my life in some way), and I realized that they were not perfect either. All of these people did the best they could with the knowledge and beliefs they had at the time when they were in my life. I made the decision to *only* keep the useful and valuable experiences that helped me to grow … and I dropped the rest. This exercise aided me in insistently changing my belief system. I have never looked back from that profound day.

Letting go of the past—whether from one minute or ten years ago—frees and opens you to new experiences, possibilities, opportunities, and relation-ships. You will discover that even your physical appearance will alter and improve. The process of releasing the vast amount of energy that has previously not been beneficial to your success in life will help you become conscious of how differently you feel by the sheer act of this release. It will help keep your mind free of thoughts that offer no benefit.

Your beliefs become your thoughts,
Your thoughts become your words,
Your words become your actions,
Your actions become your habits,
Your habits become your values,
Your values become your destiny.
— Mahatma Gandhi

ACT: To bring about a change.

Remember when you were in school and were given an assignment? The teachers were instructing you on what they wanted from you so they could be able to measure your progress or assist you in moving forward. Think of your dreams and desires as giving your mind the necessary information it needs in order to move you from lack to success. The more information you provide your mind, the easier it is for it to function positively on your behalf.

Journaling

Building on the exercises in the previous chapter, let's take it to the next step. Now that your mind is refreshed, I suggest you begin a journal listing your desires. You do not need to share this list with anyone (it's actually best if you don't). When you write about what you want, you are filling your mind with *your* unique thoughts and desires.

Exercise. Let's try this self-test: *Read* the following three words, close your eyes, and say them out loud. Notice how your body reacts.

- **Anger**
- **Depression**
- **Violence**

Okay, now write down the feelings that came across your body as you read each word. Did your body feel heavy? What colors did you notice? Were they dark or light?

Next, stand up and shake your body, an outward expression of mentally opening yourself up. Now *read* these following three words, close your eyes, and then say them out loud. Notice your body's reaction to each.

- **Smile**
- **Laugh**
- **Love**

Okay, write down the feelings that came across your body. Did your body feel lighter or possibly more relaxed? What colors did you notice? Were the colors pale or bright?

The words you use in daily life are another component of creating your path. We are all conduits of energy. The thoughts we carry, the words we speak, and the actions we take all carry energy.

Attracting Energy

The words we use express energy and attract energy to each of us. *Words, words, words ...* we use them all the time. We continue to talk, yet half the time we probably have no idea what we are truly communicating or how we end up saying the things we do. We often pay little attention to the selection of our words.

Remember, y*our choice of words has a direct effect on your life experiences . . . together, with your thoughts, you are laying the foundation for your world and your future*. Teach yourself to *think* before you speak. Notice the actual reactions of others, not what you are expecting of the situation. Ask them what they heard, so you can rephrase your thoughts if necessary.

When you use negative, self-deprecating, and self-doubting words—or words that focus on lack—you can expect that energy to return to you. Remember, like attracts like, and positive energy attracts positive energy. Same thing goes with speaking negative words.

Exercise. One of the best examples of the power of words has been shared with us by Masaru Emoto. He made a study of the effects different words, sounds, and images have on water. Please, go to YouTube, type in "Masura Emoto," and see what I'm trying to explain. I've tried it, and you may want to do the experiments yourself. Write a negative word and place it under a glass of water. Then do the same with a positive word. It does not take long to see the water particles alter depending on which word the glass of water is sitting on.

The bottom line? If you wish to create a life of success, act like a success and chose your words wisely.

Listening to Self-talk

A lifelong habit many people have created from their youth is *incorrect self-talk*. As you begin to really listen to yourself speaking, you may be surprised at the negative tone and words you are using. You may hear how you label yourself as a failure or constantly belittle yourself.

Once you identify any negative self-talk, you will need to rectify it in order to set up a positive mental atmosphere, one that will allow you to attract positive new experiences.

If you degrade yourself, your life is going to mean very little to you. If you love and appreciate yourself, then life will be fulfilling and enjoyable. I am here to tell you: Change your thinking and you can change your life.

All through your environment, place words of praise, honor, gratitude, plus any other positive words you want. Allow their energy to permeate through your environment. They need not be posted for others to see, only for you. As I have referenced through lessons gained from *Feng Shui* and Masaru Emoto, you will begin to notice changes in your environment *and* your attitude.

Become a Critical Thinker

Critical thinking is essential in creating a desirable environment. Learn to ask questions, listen to the responses, and question further. When you begin to question and ask the *'Five Ws'* (*who, what, where, when* and *why*—and sometimes *how*), you will discover that you have not really been thinking, you have only been regurgitating thoughts passed on to you without investigating the opposite thoughts or alternatives. Pay close attention and learn to question all that you are told, verbally and non-verbally, and notice how your body reacts to the information you receive.

I want to emphasize that you can either be a spectator who is led by those you let lead you; or you can become an active participant in your own life, and go in the directions you desire.

Which do you want to be?

Until you become curious and learn to question all that you have been told, you will not gain an understanding of one of the most valuable secrets of success: *Thinking*.

Exercise. A great tool I started using many years ago is to utilize the *Five Ws* whenever I learn something new. What you will discover from utilizing this process is that it will work in all aspects of your life.

Think about giving a party and preparing your invitation. You'd need to tell your invitees: *who* is having the party; *what* will occur and/or *what* they should bring to the party; *where* the party will be held; *when* the party will be held; and *why* this event is happening? Proactively utilizing the *Five Ws* removes stress for everyone. You will learn that you are discovering information that may not have initially occurred to you. In terms of this invitation example, you have laid out the facts and provided answers about every facet of your party.

What about when you are in a class or are given a job assignment? Can you see that by using the *Five Ws* you will gain clarity and feel confident you can accomplish the stated project, paper, or job assignment? Write it down in outline format. It will be easier to complete since you have asked the questions that will provide you with clarity right from the beginning.

Thinking is more fun when you begin to recognize the value of your thoughts and how they will change your life by becoming a *true thinker*.

The process of thinking is to take in information, question what you are reading, seeing, or hearing, and then digest what you need to retain. This is part of the process, but the other part of thinking is to implement the knowledge. Knowledge only becomes valuable through organization and use.

True thinkers listen as well as speak, and therefore remain aware of the circumstances around them. They have discovered that always being aware, sharing, caring, and aiding others in their lives helps to impart a sense of wellbeing. These actions provide valuable knowledge and opportunity allowing life to be lived and, in the course of living, the experiences we come across bring knowledge to our life's values.

Learn to believe. Learn to accept. Stop fighting life. Stop looking for someone on the outside to agree with you every step of your way. You must learn to think and have complete confidence in your own abilities. When you begin to develop knowledge on a variety of subjects, you will become confident in your belief or stance on a subject. But remember to remain open to the perspectives of others because, let's face it, *nobody knows everything.* By remaining flexible and open to possibilities you will attract more experiences.

We are what we repeatedly do.
Excellence, then, is not an act, but a habit.
— Aristotle

PROSPER: To put into effect your decision to change.

Reading biographies and other books on history, philosophy, art, science, even novels based on history or real life stories, will feed your mind with valuable information leading to insight. What counts in the long run is not what you read in books, but what you sift through your own mind. The ideas and impressions that are aroused in you during the process of reading—the ideas which are a reflection of your own thinking—will make you a more interesting person.

Learning to learn will open other pathways to knowledge. Important qualities of education are curiosity, interest, imagination, and a sense of the adventure in life. These are the qualities that make all learning rewarding, that make all life experiences zestful. These qualities keep us constantly seeking new experiences and deeper understanding, and enable us to continue to learn and grow during our walks through life.

It is important for you to train your mind to become capable of discovering facts, as you need them. I can't stress this enough: Train your mind by *learning* how to learn. Your brain is one of the most valuable organs you have. Think of it as an organic computer. But what isn't like a computer is when your brain functions as your mind. What you put in it is what you will get out, but with a crucial difference. It can access many facts, but facts are only part of what education is about. What you *do* with it is what matters!

Being free to read and stimulate the part of your mind that seeks further understanding is what creates self-esteem. It creates the power to discover new awareness and builds a foundation of critical thinking.

The power of thought brings great pride. Pride, used appropriately, can be a very good thing indeed. As you listen to yourself and focus your energies on your passions, desires, and self-interests, you will notice that your self-esteem will begin to grow. You will feel stronger, stand straighter, and be more willing and able to express yourself. However, you must take care not to allow your ego to become inflated and take control.

Mid-way through my life, I discovered something valuable: If I forgot about myself, did not worry about what others thought of me, and instead thought about others, I tended to feel much better about myself over all. This liberating thought gave me a strong desire to always learn what I could about others when I met them. Now, after meeting with people, I take the time to write out the key facts I learned about them for future reference. It helps me to connect with them and remember things that are relevant in their lives. They take notice of my ability to follow up with details about what is important to them. The key facts that connect us on a human level also make what happens in their lives important to me.

Connecting with others broadens our worlds and helps us move forward in life. When we live purposefully, we become living examples and inspirations for others. Engaging others while taking action in your own life; following your passions and interests; and caring for your own being can result in helping others get in touch with their passions and interests. I notice that positive efforts usually come back to me tenfold when I follow my bliss and interact with others on a regular basis. Try it and see for yourself.

Finding Balance

It is important to take care, though. Left unchecked, we can become way too busy being preoccupied and self-absorbed in our own lives. Too much self-focus on personal desires is not healthy or good for anyone. True success, however, can be ultimately created through the process of balance, by each of us caring for ourselves *and* others.

The process of knowing what you *want*, offering your knowledge, experience, and wisdom to others—and being willing to ask for what you *need* in return—gives us the tools for another important balancing act. In Matthew 7:7, *The Bible* states, "Ask and it will be given to you; seek and you will find; knock and it will be opened to you." Jesus is not talking about material things. He is talking about understanding.

Not having control of your thoughts, or what I call the *Not Knowing Syndrome*, comes from a lack of desire, curiosity, research, and willingness to spend the time investigating until you discover the answers for yourself. Until you spend your time learning, you will remain a servant of others.

It's amazing to me how many people I've come across in my life who say they *"do not know how"* to do something. People today seem to thrive on having instant access to just about every subject known to man. The *"I do not know how"* statement comes from those who have chosen a life of *lack*. These people tend to spend their lives wasting time when they could be spending that time creating their lives.

Thinking and Your Health

By now, I hope you realize that controlling your *thinking* is the key to your happiness, health, and prosperity. Indeed, through our thoughts our worlds are realized. Earlier, I offered you an exercise to help you awaken to the fact that your thoughts have a direct effect on your life. Those thoughts also have a great effect on your health. When you think negative thoughts, your body reacts to those thoughts. It follows that when words enter your mind, the body processes that energy internally to create either beneficial reactions within your organs or destructive reactions. *You choose how to implement these actions.*

Probably one of the most comprehensive and informative authors I have found on this topic is Louise Hay. Two of her books, *Heal Your Body* and *You Can Heal Your Life*, provide great insight into the power of words and the direct effect they have over health. I stumbled across these two books after years of medical challenges and a personal belief system torn between *believing I could* and *knowing I couldn't*. While reading them, I became aware of the things influencing my life: what I was hearing from others; what I was watching on television; what I was listening to on the radio; reading in books, magazines and social media; and, ultimately, the words I was using in conversation and self-talk. I had a profound revelation: *I am creating my own health issues, poor financial situation, and world of lack.* What I needed to do to remedy this was *change my thinking ...* and my health, finances, and world of lack would be filled with prosperity.

I was amazed as I witnessed just how quickly my health, financial situation, and overall life in general became positively altered. To this day, I remain conscious of the thoughts I think and the words I speak, as well as what I hear spoken around me.

I choose not to watch television or listen to the radio, nor do I bother reading information that offers no benefit to me. I recommend you NEVER go to sleep with the TV playing. This programs your mind and the programming is full of violent and negative words.

Success is truly created from your actions. Now is the time for you to decide what actions you will take, and whether those actions will lead you to the life you believe you want and deserve.

Yes, indeed, our actions are a direct reflection of our thoughts. It's the difference between something that is done and something that is stated. This reminds me of another old saying, "If you want to know who I am, don't ask me ... *watch me.*"

Success requires you identify and acknowledge your interests and passions. Once you've done that, it takes *action* to bring these desires to life. Once you begin to direct towards manifesting your interests, you'll notice that your thoughts will consistently support themselves. You'll become excited with each step you take towards accomplishing your end goals.

It's okay if you haven't yet realized you possess the power of controlling your thoughts. Until now, your thoughts have probably been controlling you. As you teach yourself to learn, you will discover your interests and passions and use them to further implement them in your life. It is truly that simple once you realize your internal dreams *can and will* help you harness the power.

Exercise. As you begin this process, recognize that your interests and passions are simply the thoughts that keep running through your mind. Like the thoughts that wake you up in the middle of the night and, no matter what you do, you just cannot stop thinking about them. Maybe the following example will better show what I mean:

When I was a teenager, I had a great longing for a coat I had seen. In my mind, I pictured myself wearing the coat. I talked to my mother about the coat, told her how beautiful I thought it was. Before going to bed each night, I would pretend to take it off and hang it in my closet. I envisioned the brilliant blue color. I felt myself sliding my hands into the warm pockets. I felt the soft lining against my skin. Guess what? Within a week, the coat was mine. What's sad about this story is that, even though I utilized the power of thought and action to get that coat, it took years before I began to consciously utilize this behavior in the rest of my life.

Ask yourself:

1. What is it that you love to do?
2. What is it that you can't wait to put your energy into?
3. What is it that you can't stop thinking about?
4. What are the rewards you can receive if you stay directed and focused on your interests?

5. Could you spend hours and hours working towards this interest, even if you were not being paid?

6. What inspires you so much that you want to tell the world about it?

Once you are ready to open your mind and recognize your true interests, it will be time to write out all the things you either wish to have or have not yet accomplished.

This list should not be composed in one sitting. Spend time on it, writing it out over days or even weeks. You will find in the process of creating your list you will begin to automatically expand your thinking. Remember, no matter what size (as big as a house?) or cost (the price of a luxury car?), the vision you place around your wants will begin to grow and evoke the concept of possibility to surround them. Also remember, the only thing that prevents you from getting your wants is a failure to take action on your beliefs.

Here are some questions to get you started:

1. What was that dream you had in grade school regarding who you wanted to grow up to be?

2. Where do you want to live and what does your house look like?

3. Are you going to become famous through your interests and talents?

4. How much money do you plan on having?

5. Do you want to travel and see the world?

6. What about marriage? Is it in your plans?

Once you begin to make your list, allow your true desires to shine and come through. During this process, you are planting the seeds of your success. It's up to you to fertilize and water your desires, nurture them. As you continue to focus on them, you will discover others will begin to surface. *NEVER* stop dreaming and taking action to create *your* world *your* way.

When I began this process, I wrote about little dreams (such as getting a new pair of shoes for work) as well as my bigger dreams (like the house and car I wanted, the relationships, owning my own business, writing books, public speaking). Personally important to me was making sure my children would be happy and I wanted happiness for myself, as well. I worked on expanding my knowledge and making connections with others who were also working at getting further in their lives. I took time to draw out my dreams, visualizing them in my mind. My list grew for weeks. I didn't expect overnight success. I nurtured my dreams and worked on realizing them.

I am pleased to share with you that I now live in the house I dreamed about. I never questioned where it would be located or how it would manifest. I own several luxury cars, have traveled to China, and have accomplished everything on every one my lists, so I continue to make lists of things I still wish to accomplish. My latest endeavors are expanding Randolph & Associates by hiring an employee who will start out in marketing and then learn how to analyze and invest clients' money; adding to my public speaking opportunities; and continuing to grow SuccessEnomics, my newest company. God works in mysterious ways (I keep saying that because it's true!) and it is up to each of us to pay attention to the signs all around us if we want to be successful.

We receive messages all throughout our lives. Many of them will be heard as negatives before we become aware that it is how we choose to hear them that really matters. You see, we can hear loving and supportive words or we can hear negative and defeating words. The choices reside within our inner-selves.

Exercise. Each day, think about what you want, where you want your life to go, and even give thought to the amount of wealth you wish to have. The more specific you are, the quicker you will notice changes in your life. Then continue to visualize and feel yourself *in your home* and *in your car*; see *yourself in a certain relationship*; picture yourself in *that particular career*; or send yourself postcards as you *travel to wherever you want to go*. Finally, notice that by thinking all these other things, you have automatically created for yourself a world of financial freedom. Whatever your desire, it *can* be manifested.

Here's the catch: You must be honest about your talents and be willing to do the work to accomplish your dreams. Naturally, it's important to remain realistic. If you're 5'5" and would like to be 6', this is not going to happen any time soon—unless you're still in puberty. Or you dream of being a concert vocalist, except you're actually tone deaf. It does not matter if you are poor, undereducated, living in an area with little opportunity, or any number of other transitory circumstances. You have the ability to not only accomplish your dreams, but also surpass them. And you can always sing your heart out in the shower!

After identifying your desires, dreams, and aspirations, you will be ready to do the work. When you are striving to complete an activity or project that brings you closer to your desired results, it should not feel like work, but a naturally flowing process.

Writing this, my latest book, brings me great joy. Inspiration for the book came to me after receiving a multitude of emails from those who attended my recent speaking engagements. I received requests to provide more information about how to manifest and realize personal success. I realized that my successes in life came only after I became well informed regarding the techniques I am sharing in this book. It took me years of study before I was able to discover that these techniques were always right in front of me. They were actually quite simple to execute. Clearly, I was the one complicating the process.

As you begin to take action towards reaching your dreams, remember, all you have to do is *know* that you are on the right track. Whatever you put into your mind is what you will attract, so it's important that you believe in your God-given talents. *No one*, and I mean *no one*, has the unique set of talents that *you* possess. Many may have similar skills, but the talents that lie within you are yours alone and they are waiting to be unleashed. These talents are what separate you from the pack. Your contribution of talents collectively, with others, helps the world move forward. *When you deny your own talents and abilities, you are also denying the world.*

It is recommended that you continue working on your dreams, talents, and skills every day in order to improve them. If you were an athlete who needed to devote long hours honing in on your talents, you would not want to wait until the day before your next big event to begin training. Successful athletes motivate and discipline themselves, spending many hours each day improving their physical skills, attitude, and thoughts. They are driven by their inner spirit.

No matter who you are, you must always continue to work on developing and strengthening your talents.

Do not wait; the time will never be 'just right.'
Start where you stand, and work with
whatever tools you may have at your command,
and better tools will be found as you go along.
— George Herbert

More Tools for Implementing What You're Learning

During the course of your life, you will hear about those who have accomplished outstanding success in sports, the arts (writing, painting, singing, acting), various fields of science, or business (investing, sales, or perhaps building a company from one core product or service into many). It doesn't matter *what* they accomplished, what's important to note here is that the majority of them were probably not geniuses. Instead, they possessed a strong *knowing* inside that drove them to become among the very best in their chosen fields.

Humility

Were you to speak with any of these people, you might be surprised to hear a consistent response, "I am not that great (or gifted or special), I just like what I do." Humility is a huge part of the real successes that ultimately stand out, make a difference, and leave a lasting footprint.

I will never forget the first time I heard someone say, "Amazing knowledge and being a genius are a waste if the knowledge is not put to use." It dawned on me that I would much rather focus and work hard at gaining knowledge, wisdom, and awareness on one or two particular subjects, as opposed to knowing only a little bit about a lot of subjects. "Jack of all trades, master of none" is a fitting cliché that underscores my point.

Hard Work

To me, *working hard* is an absolute pillar of success. Since the beginning of mankind, it has been proven over and over that those who work hard while remaining directed and focused become the leaders so many want to follow.

The idea that success is something that can be attained overnight is a fallacy. What people often notice is the evident result of an accumulation of the years of hard work, sacrifice, and belief in one's innate abilities that are often invested over a lifetime. While recognizing talent in another person is a skill and talent in its own right, it is interesting to note that when someone "discovers" a person and his or her talents, they often get most of the credit because they are the ones doing the marketing or promoting, thereby bringing the other person to the attention of the world. It only looks like overnight success because nobody ever noticed them before.

Love

The biggest key to becoming successful is to love yourself and others. Success should never be based on fame, money, and notoriety because those things are fickle and fleeting. Love lasts a lifetime.

My life had been changing for years, but it was not until I was confronted with dealing with money issues that I acknowledged the symbiotic relationships among love, peace, respect, and success. It was a very long time before I was able to look back and recognize that I was attracting the energies of success only because I spent time educating myself in all aspects of personal development, including understanding the power of the mind; the true value of wisdom (which I often found in the *Bible*); and the importance of consistently maintaining good and positive thoughts.

From the day I stepped out into the world of business, my life has moved quickly. The first day I was a receptionist at a brokerage firm, the second day I was asked to work with the top three brokers, and within less than three years I took all the exams required to become a stock broker.

By the fourth year I left a salaried position and became a stock broker making only commission. I continued to move up the ladder. In the 16th year, I opened up my own investment advisory firm, Randolph & Associates. Now, after 25-plus years, I still find great pleasure in continuing to grow within my chosen career as a Registered Investment Advisor (RIA).

As I mentioned earlier, a few years ago I wrote a book, *Randee Leads a Charmed Life*, and created a card game with one of my sisters which we called *It's SoLow*.

While attending a Freedom Fest seminar, I gave Mark Skousen (renowned economist and investment counselor) a copy of each as a gift. In response, he asked me to speak at his next year's seminar. Of course I accepted on the spot! Yet another unsolicited opportunity presented itself because I took the time and effort to give and think of someone else.

That is what action is all about. You step out, show up, expose your talent, and *voila!* more opportunities come knocking. Receiving the invitation from Mark inspired me to write the guide, *Four Secrets to Successful Investing.* That invitation also gave me the first public speaking opportunity I had received in over ten years. This opportunity energized and motivated me to continue writing and do even more public speaking. In another year and a half, I began speaking before the classes I mentioned at the beginning of this tale.

When you allow your dreams to come to life and begin to act on them, you will discover unfamiliar territories. This is because you are walking *towards* success and away from a life of lack.

Remember, life is basically quite simple, but success takes discipline, organization, and perseverance. Many obstacles will be thrown in your path, but you don't let the obstacles stop you. Though they may potentially slow you down a bit, only *you* have the power to stop yourself from achieving your goals.

Exercise. Getting started can be as simple as taking the time to make a list of what you will accomplish the next day. Begin by waking up 30 minutes or an hour earlier than usual and focus on your end result. See yourself fulfilling all of your dreams: How do you look today? How will you look in the future? What clothes are you wearing? Envision your car, home, office, and your relationships. Will you be married? Do you want to have children? What about traveling? Do you invest in the stock market, real estate, or other businesses? See it all clearly and place no limitations on your visions.

Now begin each day with the knowledge that you are already *there*, but just need to accomplish a few more things. And before you know it, you *will* be there.

Time is a relative term. Don't allow the element of time to figure into your dreams. See, feel, taste, and listen for what you desire; and your beliefs will cause the dreams to come to fruition in some form or another.

If you hear that negative chatter going on in your head: "I have to work, I have a family, no degree, I do not know anyone who can help me ...," rest assured, you *do* know people. In fact, you know plenty of people, people who are living ... or maybe not (you have access to many secrets of success left to you by those who have lived before, if you will only look for them).

Never underestimate the power of "Ask and it shall be given." Few people take the time to read motivational and business books, related magazines, and such. Nor will they take time to research or seek advice from key players in fields they wish to enter. No matter whether you elect to do your research privately or interact with others. What's important is that you reach out and ask for help, information, guidance, and take advantage of the wisdom of those who have proved they already know the secrets.

Using myself again as an example, I was divorced and raising three children with only a high school diploma. I discovered I was waking up earlier and going to bed later than I had been when I was married. Rather than complain about my lack of sleep, I used these extra hours to read and learn. I spent time reading self-help books, business magazines and books, annual reports, investment material, etc., instead of wasting time watching television (an activity, if you can call it that, which offered me no valuable insights). I spent my time filling my brain with information that would lead me to new opportunities.

When I began to change my life, I was a sales assistant making just enough money. Most of the time what I earned was not enough to take care of my family's needs. I knew I was capable of learning, so I invested my time in what I needed and wanted to learn. I gave up wasting valuable hours and turned them into productive hours.

Steps to Getting Things Done

Schedule your life. Learn to build your schedule around *you* and accomplishing your own goals. If you are not willing to do the work to change your life, you will remain a spectator who lives a poorer life. The choice is always and ultimately *yours* and yours alone. It lies within *your* decision-making process.

Get Organized. It is amazing to me how many people lose and misplace important items; or simply do not understand the value of organization. When you know where everything is and how to find it, you can save an amazing amount of time.

A friend of mine volunteers as head of an election committee for the board of a large group. He once sent me an email requesting advice on safe-guarding (i.e., not losing) their emailing list. My first thought was that he could have placed it in an Excel spreadsheet faster than the time it took to email me about it. What seemed simple to me obviously hadn't occurred to him. So, I simply copied and pasted the list into Excel, then emailed back to him with the Excel document attached. My point is, don't be one of the many people who expect others to do the small and seemingly insignificant tasks. In hindsight, I should have told him what to do and let him learn from it, because by not doing this task himself, I was keeping him from creating his own success.

This man's efforts in life too narrowly focused on making money instead of learning and applying the disciplines necessary for creating a world of prosperity. As you will discover, money isn't success; it is only a representation of the implementation of your actions. The more willing you are to take control of your thoughts and actions, it is to that degree you will enjoy the money you earn.

Don't reinvent the wheel. Today's world provides all kinds of tools to make our business life easier. Our computers and cell phones allow us to schedule meetings and create emails and contact lists and reminders and keep notes. If you still prefer twentieth century old-school tools, there are paper Day Timer calendar journals which can be used. I recently saw a business accessories catalog with updated versions of this once handy tool. Either method requires just a bit of skill to utilize your equipment. Ask yourself: What is preventing me from simplifying my life?

Develop your small skills. Thinking, defining your desires, and acting upon them are secrets of becoming successful. Pay close attention to the details. The *small skills* that may seem boring, mundane, and cause you to feel aggravated are usually very important. Instead of pushing them aside, seek solutions to learn them. It's in these details that you will find the components which often separate the winners from the losers.

You're probably thinking, "What *small skills?*" To begin with, let's talk about basic office skills. In today's world of computers and smartphones, etc., few will take the time to understand the sophisticated technologies that drive the tools people use daily. They often avoid learning even the most basic computer skills that would ultimately set them apart from the crowd and make lives so much easier.

Many people only learn how to search the Web, send and receive emails, compose letters, and maybe a few more learn how to use a spreadsheet program. Regarding cell phones, most only use a fraction of the technology that is literally at their fingertips.

If you desire to automate your life and make it simpler, make the effort of either taking classes or have a friend (or one of your children!) help educate you. Don't be shy about walking into the store that sold you your cell phone and having them explain and demonstrate the functions and technology you do not understand.

Filing, the other F word. It is important to be able to locate pertinent documentation when it's needed. This applies to both personal and professional documents. Accordingly, it is important to have a system to know how to file away the hardcopy documents, as well as creating electronic files and folders. It's a simple habit to acquire, so learn to do it as you go and you'll be amazed at the results.

Scheduling appointments, recording contacts, and saving valuable documents in folders are all important functions and every business owner's responsibility. Whether you are the employer or employee, it's important to learn how to keep your documents for clients and prospects well organized. This skill can be utilized at home removing stress from your personal environment.

Some of you may remember the early dotcom boom and how they told us paper would be eliminated by the twenty-first century? Well, the paper world is not gone yet and there are many times you will find it imperative that you provide hardcopy documentation in order to prove and defend your position. Keep this in mind: Many attorneys expect to win cases because they count on so many of you not keeping accurate records.

A pile becomes a file. See that pile of papers on your desk? Did you know that by turning them vertically instead of leaving them stacked horizontally you will have created a file? All you have to do is sort them into folders with handwritten labels (no need to waste time with printed ones, unless you're compulsive about such things). When you're done, you may feel so good about it that you'll go back and sort what's inside those folders into chronological order or topics.

I know how distasteful and time-consuming this extra work may sound to you. However, I promise you that a substantial part of my success is based on the fact I keep my records and affairs in order, exactly as I have been recommending for you. Do not fight these menial tasks; ironically, they will empower you. Learn to do them, take assurance that familiarity with them will have rewards, and discover that you have freed your mind, reduced stress in your life, and gained peace of mind when you know you can get your hands on your information quickly and easily. By the way, this really impresses the heck out of others and helps you gain respect.

Networking. Once you begin researching and studying people in your chosen field(s) of interest, you are on the path and there is no turning back. You begin reaching out, asking the Universe for help, and making connections with those who, like you, are actively pursuing their own successes. You do not need to be concerned that you will fail because once you start you *cannot* fail. For you will have discovered it is not the end result that matters. It is all about the journey and the process; it's the *doing* that brings love, pleasure, and respect to your life.

Continue to expand your relationships and attend events that keep you out of your comfort zone. Stretch your knowledge base into areas that are needed in your world but may be foreign to your thinking. You see, at some point … before you know it … you will realize you have gained an immense amount of knowledge, the kind you can *use*.

Take the time to develop a network of people with whom you can reach out and offer your assistance. Through offering your knowledge, wisdom, and insight, you are revealing your talents to them. This creates a desire within them to connect with you as well. As you assist them, you will begin to build a meaningful and mutually beneficial relationship which may even expand from the business world into your personal life.

Look like you feel … or feel like you look. Your attitude and attire project *who* you are on the inside. However, you may need to be prepared to alter your outer appearance even though your inner self isn't quite there yet. Reflect who you wish to be while in the process of learning to become that person.

True, life-altering changes begin on the inside, first in your thoughts and then in your heart and soul. You can aid in this transformation by simply updating your external you.

Always wear a smile and be pleasant. Immediately upon introduction, ask questions about the person you have just met. Asking questions means that you are willing to listen, so make sure you do! Learn as much as you can about them, keep the conversation on who they are, what they do, their businesses, and you will be surprised at their reactions. They will walk away being intrigued by you and thinking more about you than you could ever believe. Why? Because you made them feel important, valued, and respected.

There is an old saying, "You can catch more flies with honey than you can with vinegar." Being nice, kind, and respectful will bring you more rewards than being rude, angry, and self-serving.

Memory problems? Maybe you keep quiet because you think you can't remember their names let alone anything pertinent about them. If you think you need a trick to help you remember, there are many effective books on building your memory, so add one to your library of self-help books for future reading.

In the meantime, once you gain knowledge about someone, you will want to record it in the address book of your computer or smartphone. When meeting someone for the first time, be sure to exchange business cards. You can jot down vital information on the back. That's okay to do in front of them, it shows you are sincere about knowing them. Or you can wait until you've parted company, whatever works best for your personal style.

Next, send them a follow-up note that again focuses on what you've learned about them. Don't be gushy or sound like a stalker. Keep it simple and genuine.

On the third connection with that person you should be asking to meet them for coffee, lunch, or dinner, depending on your comfort level and what is appropriate for the situation. The third meeting is when you can share about yourself. This is how to build meaningful relationships.

Whether this is personal or business, you should always make good impressions and work to make connections. Learn how to appropriately represent yourself and your company. Remain aware of what is occurring in the community or country with regard to your prospect's or client's companies. Forwarding them information they may not be aware of shows you care because you have taken the time to learn about them, their businesses, and their companies.

When someone sends you a referral, always send a thank you note or tell him or her personally how much you appreciate the gesture. Think of how you would like to be treated and treat others the same way. It is always the kind, human actions that bring positive attention to you.

Correspondence. Mail can be a good thing or overwhelming, whether email or physical. When you open an email and read it, take any action that may be required at that time. This may be providing a response to an invite, placing into the junk file, creating a rule in your computer to prevent receiving further information from a certain party, or just deleting it; but do what needs to be done at that time. If this is an important communication you may need to reference at a later date, *save it in a file*. You may need to create a new folder, so make sure you give it a name you would easily be able to reference in the future. It could even be the name of the person who sent it, if you know they will be your main contact, or perhaps the name of the project. No matter what you call the folder, you will want to keep it simple and mentally connected to the file name. Be sure to put your replies in that file as well. Do not leave the computer until you have completed all that is required.

Touch it once. Snail mail requires a similar action. A powerful time management tool is to only touch a piece of paper once: open, read, write a response, file or discard (shred/recyle), and move on. Too many times people open an important letter, then get distracted and forget to respond. You will discover stress is reduced from your life simply by taking immediate action.

The mind is interesting. It can function very well and become your best friend if you will respect its ability to function. Remaining focused, self-directed, and completing whatever conversation, project, or assignment you are working on, prior to moving to the next one, will add to your success. It will ultimately increase your pride and self-respect, as you no longer need to clutter your mind with uncompleted items on your list.

If you have been implementing the exercises in this book, by now your thoughts should be clarifying your dreams and, hopefully, you are noticing that your body is feeling lighter, with feelings of success replacing feelings of failure, and that doubtful image you used to project all around you. Your spirit has begun to come alive and your energy is creating more energy. You are invigorated. This *new you* is replacing the *lazy doubter* who once lived within.

What we really want to do is what we are really meant to do.
When we do what we are meant to do, money comes to us,
doors open for us, we feel useful, and the work we do
feels like play to us." —Julia Cameron

Money and Wealth

You have learned how to bring life to your dreams and have begun to take action. But money, where will the money come from to implement your dream? Simply, right from where it is now.

Dreamers are risk takers. They have discovered their power lies within and it is up to them to create the opportunities which will allow them to see their dreams come true, all while enjoying the fruits of their labor.

"Wait," you say, "I have no money to spare."

If you have no money to spare, then how have you been using your creative thinking? Money is only a reward given to you for the actions you have taken. Have you only half-heartedly given of your talents? Or have you made good money but have financially over-obligated yourself? Or perhaps have you just been wasteful with your funds?

Your self beliefs had to be altered in order to allow you to release your dreams and begin to take actions on creating them. Now it is time to alter your beliefs regarding money.

Money is simply an exchange between people for goods or services which have been produced. Nothing more, nothing less. It is as simple as this: you work and you are given money in exchange for your work. Perhaps it is your attitude or belief regarding money which needs to be altered.

Wealth is not created by making millions. It is created like everything else in your life; that is, through respect, knowledge, and putting a little to the side each paycheck.

Many of you reading this book may be working for or have worked at a company which has a 401k retirement plan. Or you may be with or have worked at a union which automatically takes a portion from your paycheck to save for you. What about the Social Security deductions coming out of your checks? This is an example of a forced way that money is saved for you; however, it offers you little security. I say this because you are the only one who should be in control of your money. With Social Security alone you are allowing the government to be in control of your future. It is your responsibility to understand the basics of how money functions and the benefits which you can derive from this understanding.

Saving is as simple as this: You receive a check and place a percentage, say 10%, away into an account. You may or may not earn much interest on these funds while they sit there. However, at the beginning, this should not concern you. You need to develop a new belief of the value of your money and create new habits regarding money. You are practicing money management, and we all know practice makes perfect.

Money will work hard for you once YOU discover that it can be your employee. As you save you will begin to feel different, more secure in your decision making, which will develop into wanting your money to work harder than it would just in a savings account. After you have built up a nice reserve, you will then need to begin to invest some into securities. This is when your invested money can act as your own employee, working for you while you continue on your life's path. As with any other employee, you will need to be observant and make alterations until you are comfortable the money is doing the job you were hoping for. Investing is no different than dating. In dating you need to take the time to get to know the person, where they came from, what they want out of life, etc. This is how you discover if you wish to continue to spend time with this person. A similar principle lies in investing. Where and when did the company begin? Do you like the product or service they offer? Has management changed a lot? In other words, will you stay with this company in good times and bad?

Compounding Your Way of Thinking

Before I go on, I want to share with you a little-discussed fact about the power of compounding. Compounding in the financial world means "to pay interest on both an amount of money and the interest it has already earned." In other words, when your money makes money you can leave that in the pot and your original investment as well as the earnings made can now work for you. You probably are saying, "Okay, but I don't have thousands to invest so why should I care?"

Here is a true fact and I want you to let it sink in so you can get a firm understanding of how a little today will give you a lot tomorrow—as long as you continue to allow your money to work and do not interrupt its course, but add to it.

Imagine if someone offered to give you a penny and then would double it each day. They start with one penny, then the next day two, then four, eight, sixteen, thirty two, and so on. How much money would they have to give you in 30 days? Try and think this out before you look at the answer.

Ready? It is $5,368,709.12!

That is the power of compounding. If you will simply save 10% each pay check, then begin to allow your money to work by investing in good quality stocks for the long run you will discover you are creating your own compounding power, not quite as startling as the table on the next page, but you'll still be amazed!

Double a Penny Every Day for 30 Days

Day 1:	$.01	Day 11:	$10.24	Day 21:	$10,485.76
Day 2:	.02	Day 12:	20.48	Day 22:	20,971.52
Day 3:	.04	Day 13:	40.96	Day 23:	41,943.04
Day 4:	.08	Day 11:	81.92	Day 24:	83,886.08
Day 5:	.16	Day 15:	163.84	Day 25:	167,772.16
Day 6:	.32	Day 16:	327.68	Day 26:	335,544.32
Day 7:	.64	Day 17:	655.36	Day 27:	671,088.64
Day 8:	1.28	Day 18:	1,310.72	Day 28:	1,342,177.28
Day 9:	2.56	Day 19:	2,621.44	Day 29:	2,684,354.56
Day 10:	5.12	Day 20:	5,242.88	Day 30:	5,368,709.12

I began this book talking about the power of your words and thoughts and how, by changing them, your life will in turn change and you will see and hear your life differently. You will need to replace all your doubting thoughts with ones of belief, in yourself and in your abilities, and take action to make them come true. That same process continues through every aspect of your life.

Change your thoughts and you will change your life.

Change your habits and beliefs regarding money and you will create financial freedom. So, the question now becomes, "Are you willing to take responsibility for your own financial freedom?"

Exercise. I wish for you to take the time to journal and write about your money beliefs. Do you know if you created your belief or were you told to see money in a negative way? Over your lifetime, you have no doubt heard thousands of comments about money and observed the money behavior of the people closest to you, your parents, friends, relatives, teachers, or colleagues. Their comments regarding money were reinforced through your continual beliefs which now lie in your subconscious thinking. You can break this cycle. You are the only one who has the power to replace negative thoughts and feelings with positive thoughts and feelings that create the results you seek.

You start by creating the habit of saving a percentage of each pay check you receive, in addition to any type of retirement money that is being taken out of your paycheck. You need to build a financial reserve which will cover one year of overhead expenses (house payment/rent, utilities, car payment, insurance, food, other payments such as student loans, etc.).

Always live on cash. Bank debit cards can help with this. *Never use credit cards* unless you know you can pay the balance in full every month.

You will soon discover that your attitude of life is improving and your new habits have not prevented you from enjoying life. Life is happier when you love and respect yourself. This will be easily reflected through how much you are putting away towards your future dreams, coaxing them into fruition.

Your Talent Pool

Now that you are in the habit of saving, you will need to continue to expand your knowledge and build on your relationships. You need to continually learn about your fields of interest, but also expand your talent pool. Discover who can aid you in gaining knowledge in areas you need to understand but in which you have little interest.

Your talent pool will become full of people whom you will be able to assist in accordance to their needs, just as they share their talents with you. Many times this process is referred to as networking.

Networking means little or nothing if you don't *use* the talents from the pools with which you have become involved.

Here's a little secret: We all love to strut ourselves and are honored when we can give assistance to others. Giving is part of the enjoyment of life. So, never be afraid to give of your time and your talents when others need your help.

Discover Your Money Character

You have become comfortable with your savings, are watching it expand, and you are thinking that it is time to look into investing. However, that inner voice of yours might be telling you that you should not invest. You know you will soon have money to invest, but you do not want to lose it.

The time has come to discover your money character, that is, how you see and feel about investing your money. Below are questions to ask yourself in order to understand how you think about money and investing. Your answers will help you recognize which of your beliefs need to be altered and will educate you to the benefits of having your money work for you. (Pencil in your replies in the space left after each question so you can come back to them later.)

- Do you understand what the stock market is and what you can expect to achieve by investing?

- Are you equally aware of the market's limitations in helping you toward achieving your goals?

- Can you afford the money and time to become and remain informed about your investments, and do you want to? (If your reply is affirmative, be certain that the "you" is neither the collective you described in advertising targeted at the inexperienced investor, nor the "you" someone else thinks *should* be investing.)

- Are you basically optimistic?
  (Pessimists usually have a difficult time in the stock market.)

- Do you tend to easily worry about things?
  (If so, you probably have enough to worry about without letting the market's ups and downs further traumatize your psyche.)

- Can you resist going along with popular fads?

- Do you like to follow the crowd?

- Does money quickly burn a hole in your pocket?

- Do you recognize that you will never be a complete "master of your fate" in the market?

- Do you realize is it likely you will never be the one who will buy at the bottom or sell at the top?

- Can you use your experience in other activities to help guide you in determining whether you should invest in the stock market?

  (Do you plan, are you focused, flexible, patient, etc.?)

- How well do you work with other professionals?

- Have you worked hard for a political candidate who lost? (How did it affect you emotionally, especially in regards to further political activities?)

- If you hired a professional to do construction or build an addition to your home, was it generally a pleasant experience? Was the result enjoyable and satisfying? Or was it stressful?

- If you have ever lost money gambling in a casino, how did you feel afterward? Have you been back since?

- When unexpected events prevent the execution of a carefully developed plan, are you able to accept reasonably well the need to modify your plan?

The questions above will help you to recognize your money character. In other words: the way you feel and see yourself when it comes to money. Another approach which may be of value in discovering your money character and ability to take risks is to identify your dreams.

- Do you want your money to grow, but have no interest in watching the markets, and the markets actually scare you? If so, you may be a mutual fund buyer.

- Do you want to own your own company? This dream usually designates a person who has a risk personality as long as the odds are in their favor. They typically become long term investors, but are willing to buy into younger companies.

- If you like fast driving and enjoy dangerous sports, then you may be a *high risk taker*, which means you probably have more interest in trading versus investing in the markets.

Ask others how they view you and why, and see if their impressions aid you in identifying your own money character.

Keep in mind the value in understanding your own money character early on:

- You will be able to invest *your* way rather than how others tell you to.
- Stress is removed as you see your money working for you.

Early in my life I stepped into investing in the stock market; however, I was young and needed the money so I sold my stock and used the income towards my education. My next opportunity came in real estate. I actually became a licensed realtor, but found I had little interest in selling or investing my money in real estate.

As I shared earlier, years later Fate led me—as it often does if you're paying attention to the signs—to a dual opportunity. Not only did I physically step through the doors into working at a stock brokerage firm, but I was prompted into recalling my earlier experience of investing in stocks. I knew that my money character was inclined towards discovering opportunities early and staying focused on their outcome over the years. Vision must be tempered with patience for this to work. That is why I not only invest in stocks but continue to this day working with those who have made it, and then with those who *wish to make it* in the world of stock investing. If you come away with nothing else, let it be this: **Become a Lifelong Investor.**

Taking the time to truly know your money character prior to placing money in real estate, your own company, or the stock market will save you time and emotional stress. Please take the time to discover YOUR money character.

Always remember, your success comes through your own thoughts, taking action to bringing your dreams to fruition, and implementing the needed steps to create your life of success.

Create as much wealth as your heart desires. Surround yourself with beauty, spend the wealth, and share it by giving to others … your family, friends, and/or the world. Wealth is only energy. All you need to do is give your attention to affluence and it will automatically be attracted to you.

Put a smile on your face, recognize the *inner knowing* that already resides inside you, feel your spirit, and believe that the time has arrived for *YOU* to have all your dreams and desires come to life.

If you wish to learn more about becoming a Lifelong Investor, email vicki@randolphassociates.net and discover how I can help you realize all this book has to offer.

I wish you health, patience, success, and your heart's desires. Now, go on and write your own beautiful and unique life's story!

About the Author

 Like many young women of her generation, Vicki L. Wille had visions of a traditional life as a wife, mother, and homemaker. Her life's path began with every expectation of fulfilling that vision. That path took a turn in an entirely different direction when her marriage ended.

Now single and a young mother of three, Vicki drew upon her Midwestern heritage. She took the necessary steps to successfully balance family priority, professional responsibilities, and personal fulfillment.

The course of Vicki's personal and professional development is truly inspiring. Her strong work ethic and commitment to client satisfaction propelled her from an entry level sales assistant position to an award winning broker, ultimately becoming a Registered Investment Advisor and Owner/Principal at Randolph & Associates. Since opening her firm in 2000, she has managed the financial portfolios and created wealth for many high net-worth clients.

She developed a card game called *It's SoLow* which has been reported to assist in creating social connections within families while aiding in the improvement of math and critical thinking skills. She wrote *Randee Leads a Charmed Life* (penned under her maiden name, Vicki Silberberger), a collection of parables illustrating ways to live life to its fullest by honoring family tradition and recognizing that positive, life changing gifts often come disguised as adversities. She also wrote *Four Secrets to Successful Investing*, a primer that can make anyone a smarter investor.

Vicki's commitment to community service, and her belief in critical thinking and living a deliberate life, has led her to once again share her life experiences with others. With a passion to assist those working to create their own success, her most recent endeavor is SuccessEnomics. In an effort to create self-fulfillment and financial freedom, this 'Community of Thinkers' utilizes Vicki's strategy and insight to reach new heights in all facets of their lives.

Her inspiring message resonates with audiences of all ages and backgrounds. Create your own destiny and join Vicki Wille's Community of Thinkers!

To book Vicki Wille for your next event, fundraiser, or to invite her to speak at your school or upcoming civic meeting, please email Vicki@SuccessEnomics.com or call 702-370-3998. For pricing information please visit SuccessEnomics.com.

Changing the Lives of MILLIONS from 'Lack to Prosperity' by Seeing and Hearing Life Differently

Acknowledgements

Special thanks go to my developmental editor, Molly Aine Moore, who was not afraid to offer her principles and challenged me all along the way. She was not only helpful with all forms of editing and rewrites, but also with the tricky minutia of self-publishing. Her input has been invaluable.

During the course of this project, Molly offered her help with other aspects of my business—which led to her becoming my virtual assistant. Added to her dependable work ethics, her insight, life-experiences, and knowledge of varied aspects of conducting business virtually (websites, newsletters, desktop publishing, printing, newsletters, social media, plus basic advertising and marketing) have aided me in my financial company as well as my book writing and public speaking.